Coming Out
  Coming to Faith
Coming to the Table

FIRST BE RECONCILED

Coming Out
Coming to Faith
Coming to the Table

Stories We Told Across Enemy Lines

PEGGY GREEN, M.Div.

FOREWORD BY RIESS POTTERVELD, PhD

PEGGY GREEN PRESS
SAN FRANCISCO

Coming Out, Coming to Faith, Coming to the Table:
Stories We Told Across Enemy Lines
published by Peggy Green Press, St. Petersburg, Florida

Printed in the United States of America
First printing December 2014

ISBN: 978-0-9863142-0-9

Cover and text design by Drew Stevens, studiodrew.net
Proofreading by Deanna Horner
Co-editing by Faith Jansen and Peggy Green

The ideas herein are the personal views and representations of the
author and speakers, and have not been endorsed by their churches,
denominations or by any other person or group.

For inquiries and permissions, contact the author:
P.O. Box 1835
St. Petersburg, FL 33731
Info@PeggyGreen.net

For Debi

Contents

Foreword

One of the joys of reading is the invitation to look deeply into fictional lives, not as voyeurs but as fellow human beings searching to expand our own experience and learning. Often, we discover that our habituated way of taking in the world is too narrow, too constrained, and in need of disruption and expansion. Peggy Green, in her remarkable book, *Coming Out, Coming to Faith, Coming to the Table,* has allowed us access to real living people, who over an extended period of time, engaged each other in deep and probing conversations. The richness of this book lies in its power to invoke transformative change by allowing us access to the experiences of others who have walked a different path.

From the very beginning we are forewarned that these sessions of speaking and listening will focus on tough issues that involve sexual orientation and gender identity, differing views of biblical authority and divergence in interpretation of unsettling Biblical texts, not to mention fractured family dynamics and human alienation, as well as moments of healing, reconciliation and self-discovery.

The participants in this experiment were chosen not to ensure harmony but to stimulate divergence of viewpoint at the risk of potential hostility. But the participants agreed that there was value in encountering the "other." Employing Appreciative Inquiry and a host of other peace-building tools, they came to "First Be Reconciled" fully prepared to engage the discomfort of "culture wars." How deeply appreciative we are that these strangers chose to join this extended chorus and were willing to have their life experiences placed into print.

At times, these entries reminded me of the self-disclosing letters people used to write with pen and paper, placing their deepest and most anguished observations into letters sent by horseback and sailing ship to intimates who could be trusted with shared personal knowledge. Even though the passages in this book are spoken conversation, the reader feels that the speakers are truly diving deep to touch on feelings, fears, and experiences that shaped their personal lives. The passages contain intimate disclosures.

Never straight lines, the stories have the locomotion of back and forth conversation. And they are short enough that we remember the insights that emerge and carry them with us as we move from one speaker to another. Wisdom accumulates as we piece together distinct experiences that share commonalities. The reader is charged with the task of parsing out what can be learned from the witness of each guide.

There is evidence surely in this book of the real pain imposed by the marginalization of gay and lesbian people within some portions of the Christian community and within certain cultures that express hostility towards behavior deemed outside of the norm.

Some participants give testimony of a transformation in their previous beliefs. And some give testimony to the fact that honest conversation can bring healing and reconciliation.

I have noted how people on the move, walking down the street or riding the subway, are listening to music through earpieces or texting frantically into their cell phones. Somewhere I read about three girls sitting on a bench texting like crazy to their friends who were sitting nearby. Maybe we don't very often have the kind of conversations revealed in this book? Reading this book made me feel a hunger for the kind of conversation and storytelling that requires time, transparency, vulnerability, and honesty.

I wanted to ask the participants if, after First Be Reconciled, they'd found other people with whom to expand upon this dialogue of self-revelation and self-discovery. Did the things other people said, or that they themselves had said, come back to leaven future experiences and encounters? Having read this book, I am sure it will be true for me—the words and stories will visit me again.

Riess W. Potterveld
President, Graduate Theological Union

Author's Note

Transcripts: The stories told in these pages, taken from the transcripts of recorded dialogue, have been edited for clarity and brevity.

Privacy: Unless they have granted permission to use their real names, to protect the privacy and confidentiality of the people in this book, the names of the speakers and subjects, as well as the names of those they've discussed, have been changed. Some identifying facts have been changed and replaced with fictional information for the same reason.

How to Read This Book

There are two kinds of stories in this book: one very brief memoir in two parts, and several dozen very short stories. Although you could read these stories in any order you want to, you'll get much more out of it if you read the stories in the order presented. Here's why:

While *The Prodigal Daughter* occurred before the project First Be Reconciled, *The Prodigal Daughter's Son*, which happened after, was directly influenced by First Be Reconciled.

The stories, the storytellers and their relationships evolve. This progression is best experienced by reading the stories in the order presented.

Introduction

O n the battlefield between Left and Right, *First Be Reconciled* is conversation between American factions that don't speak the same language. At the Gettysburg of our civil war, we speak Justice or Promise; we speak Marriage Equality or Biblical Infallibility; we cite polls and prophets, preachers and poets, and we talk each other into a coma.

Yet, all the while, as the Right speaks "Family" and the Left speaks "Community," we are reaching for the heart of humanity. While the Right speaks "Dominion" and the Left speaks "Communion," the heart of humanity is reaching for divinity. On the battlefield between Left and Right, where we still sing, *This Land is your land, this land is my land,*[1] we still have this American dream.

But some say we're running out of time.

Call it Climate Change or Judgment Day; blame the collapse of the traditional family or the greed of the One Percent. Whether you plan to be sucked up in a rapture, beamed up by Scotty, or fully present in the moment, First Be Reconciled is an opportunity to experience the reason why some variation of the word "forgive" is found nearly fifty times in the New Testament alone—and found over half that time in the mouth of Jesus. I have to think he was up to something. I have to ask, *What did he want?* First Be Reconciled is an invitation to members of two warring tribes to step together into the heart of that question.

The week before Nine-Eleven, First Be Reconciled set out on a mission: to build trust and foster working relationships between culture warriors. To build trust, we begin with a common language—in this case, the language of faith. To foster working relationships, we balance the comfort of shared language with the challenge of shared leadership. Each reconciler is required to co-facilitate with an opponent.

With the support of Pacific School of Religion, the Graduate Theological Union, and the E. Rhodes and Leona B. Carpenter Foundation, First Be Reconciled (FBR) between 2001 and 2004, brought together seven groups and facilitated dozens of "one-on-one" dialogues.

In FBR, where we neither seek agreement on the issues that divide us, nor silence the voices of the values that define us, we seek, as a group, to become an instrument of peace. We sit, by the windows of the soul, tracing the steps of the divine journey through the fires and the waters of our own lives.

There—apart from rhetoric, aside from stereotypes, just beneath these scary labels—are stories: a tale of transformation, a journey of faith, a road to recovery, a moment of truth. Each of us has left the lamp behind a bushel; each of us has stepped into the light.

Call it dialogue but it's more than that. Call it peace-making, skill-building, storytelling; it's all of that. But what if that's not what I'm after?

If what I'm after goes deeper than that; if what I want is freedom from my own resentment; if what I want is emancipation from my own anger and my own blame—then maybe this practice is right on target. And maybe these people are just the ticket.

How will we learn to live with our differences? In FBR, where we enter the process seeking understanding, we leave the process having made decisions with, and having co-facilitated with, someone with whom we disagree. This, as we move from hearing each other to working together, is where the rubber meets the road. This is where adversaries reach agreements, build agendas, and take the stage.

This, the work of reconciliation, is one place to pass the cup—and have a taste—of the peace that "surpasses all understanding."[2]

首先和解

First be reconciled

The Prodigal Daughter

Home, I said.
In every language there is a word for it . . . .
                    —Mary Oliver, *The River*

Prologue

Have you ever stood, leaning into the sky, as a single fish, condensing her scales on some invisible coil, disappeared beneath the white lather only to spring, headlong, into a wall of crashing river? Have you ever stood, breath suspended, while she, somewhere under that vortex of foam, wound herself up like a rubber band airplane, and propelled herself into the dam? Did you notice how she never stopped, mid-leap, to say, *Screw this*; how she never turned back to ask if she shouldn't have her head examined?

When I think of gay people and evangelicals, moving past the cold and narrow images we hold of one another, towards the warm and spacious faces we often find across the table, when I think of the perilous move to make amends, I think of that mystical fish, launching over the dam, leaping towards the end of her life, doing the one thing she has to do in order to call herself Salmon.

When I think of that disciplined sprinter, battered and bruised, exhausted and depleted, finally reaching those rock-a-bye ripples—where new life squirms barely born in the stream, where old life floats belly-up towards the sea—I think of the role of death in the reconciling journey. When I think of the salmon, falling back on the clear water forever, when I remember that the word sacrifice means "to make holy," I think of the role of forgiveness in the death of the very self that stands between the belly-up and the barely born.

And that, of course, is why you rarely hear about people breaking down doors in order to forgive.

Moreover, it is one thing to forgive a single person a single act. It is quite another to forgive an entire caste system for that "deepest cut" that repeats itself day in and day out. Somehow identity forms, like the scar above a wound, around those acts of everyday betrayal. It is one thing to put aside a single bad memory. But to put aside the defended self, to release this "I," battered and bruised, back to the sea—that is the longing of the body for the soul. That is the singing of the many to the One.

But that doesn't mean, to the separated self, to the armed guard called "me alone," that this head-banging, hunger-striking upstream migration, hundreds of miles long, is anything less than an obstacle course full of saber-tooth nets and predatory lips.

And yet, to the layer of the journey that is best understood as an act of community, the move to release this me back to the sea can be a thing of practical joy. And all it takes is *ears to hear*.[3] So take heart. But leave everything else behind. As with the salmon, vaulting over the dam, deep in the DNA of the prodigal daughter and the prodigal son, there is a compass, there is a map, there is a way to get back home.

Is There Anybody
You Need to Forgive?

He pitched a fast glance across the blanket and pleaded, "Why does it take so long to die?" And the priest, who'd faithfully tucked Communion into his side pocket, felt a steady breath expand his belly as he stepped forward carefully. Without a hint of "the old routine" that was due such a veteran of the upcoming conversation, he hoisted a chair on the tip of his toe and quietly slipped it closer in.

"Mike," he began, "heaven is not a house of bitterness."

Until his daily pack of Lucky Strikes struck out both lungs, and finally dumped him in the dugout of "permanent disability," the old man, our grandfather, was a cop. Although we never actually saw him in blue, we knew: during the Great Depression, he had a job; in his City by the Bay, he walked a beat—past the women in bandanas waiting for the trolley, past the men off the freight trains standing in the soup line.

An officer of the law, Michael Murray liked order: he respected authority, he liked clothing that made one's station clear, he liked everyone (and everything) to know its place and stay there. When, long after he'd retired, the height requirement was lowered, making it possible for "fruits, dwarfs and Chinamen" to join the Force, it was a chop to the kneecap of the six-foot Sergeant Murray.

And when the sisters' hems were raised—their habits modified—making it possible for everything from bangs to varicose veins to stick out unashamed, it was (after the 300 years it took the Vatican to enter the age that everyone else was leaving behind) too much too soon for "Yabbo." That's what we called him—still do—when we were too little to say "Grandpa."

Irish as he was Catholic, you could say our grandfather was devout: he loved the Church; he loved the Mass; he loved the Father, the Son, and the Holy Ghost. He believed, until his dying breath, that Baptism (so long as it occurred in the Holy Roman Catholic Church) meant (so long as the baptized kept the Commandments and otherwise went to Confession) that the baptized would go to heaven.

"But," the priest seemed to be saying, there was more to it than the 'shalts,' the Sacraments, and the 'shalt nots.' There was the truly holy human spirit: there was the heart free of anger and hate, free of the harm we returned to the ones who'd brought us hurt. Two hands opened to a brother Catholic who was clutching at Jesus and gasping for air, a good priest, head down, leaned in. "Is there anybody you need to forgive?"

· · ·

My sister Molly, who says of our grandparents, "I really loved Nonna and Yabbo," was once an ordinary fan of Joni Mitchell and Bob Dylan. Although she was never inclined to Tune in, Turn on, and Drop out, she did whack another path, way-clean of the mainstream, when she became a "Jesus freak" at the age of nineteen.

On the heels of her entrance into unwed motherhood, and all of its attendant humiliations and losses, she drifted towards a band of believers rumored to have followed their apostle from the desert sands to the urban badlands to the Mexican jungles—and back.

Nonna, renowned from Kearny Street to County Cork for the curative properties of her lamb stew (which went down especially nice with a pint of home brew), had a never-ending supply of both of them and a way of divining just which grandchild would be calling up in search of "medicine."

Nonna was just rehearsing her response, "Just steppin' out, y' know; pretty busy this week," as Molly called to claim a bowl of her birthright. In order to keep Molly and her baby out of the path (and out of the wrath) of Yabbo, Nonna did what she had to do.

When somehow it happened that Baby Zoe became a known entity to Yabbo, he not only refused to see the two of them, but he banned both of them from his beat entirely. Years later, when it appeared that Yabbo wasn't long for this world, Molly had to tiptoe into the backyard if she wanted to visit Nonna.

Before Yabbo's final decline, back when Nonna felt okay about leaving Yabbo home alone, Nonna used to meet Molly, and one of her ever-expanding flock of home-schooled children, downtown. (It wasn't only that she wasn't married in the One True Church; it was also the fact that no "real priest" had ever baptized a one of those little kids, not Zoe, not Zachary, not any of them—damned to the last one by the misguided choices of their Bible-banging mother.)

Even after Molly had "cleaned up," got married (married to the guy who not only carried that tiny Zoe on his back through her first mind-meld with the Pacific Ocean—but would, eventually, do the same for Zachary and the twelve other children he would raise with my sister), Yabbo refused to acknowledge her.

In what became the first real searing knife of her

adult life, a devout Catholic had used his faith to tell his own flesh and blood that she and her Bible weren't good enough for God. With that, he locked her out of his house and out of his heart. Within a couple of years, he would do the same thing, for the same UnCatholic treason, to my cousin Brendan. It was an act that brought my cousin to the bones of his knees and nearly shattered them.

• • •

It happened somewhere between two things: Anita Bryant's campaign to catapult the gay movement onto the political landscape; and Dan White's murders of San Francisco Mayor George Moscone and Supervisor Harvey Milk—after which, with all the courage of a deer in head-lights, I went home and came out to my parents. I was almost twenty-one.

Suffice it to say, it was New Year's Day, 1979. In the last house in which we would all live together, all four kids were back home in the 'burbs. It was late in the afternoon—I was down in the laundry room with a stack of Levi's 501s—when I heard my sister call my name.

Up the stairs and down the hall, over carpet the

color of the perfect front lawn, I entered the room I once shared with my sister.

On the bed that first belonged to Nonna and Yabbo, as Zoe lay kicking on the old wool blanket, Molly's Bible lay wide awake inside the little sleeper she'd made for it. It was then that I noticed that her Bible was open—and coming towards me like a car I knew was going to hit me.

In the spot where her finger would impale that scripture straight through my hand, was the book that called "vile affections" that which threatened the "natural use" of the woman.[4] It happened then. When I didn't scream and I couldn't cry; when I didn't slam the book down and couldn't toss a hot grenade across the room.

A slice of Christian faith so penetrating in scope, I dreamt that night of the Iron Maiden in which young girls were skewered until they renounced Satan. In what became the first searing knife of my adult life, an evangelical had used her bible to tell her sister that God couldn't love her quite the way she was.

• • •

In lingering memories of things Molly told me in the years after Yabbo died, Yabbo said Yes to that priest. He could hardly breathe and he could barely speak;

yet, one way or another, Yabbo did say, "My grand-daughter . . . I can forgive Molly."

In lingering memories of things she'd told me—of how she'd gone and sat at his bedside, and how Yabbo spoke his ten years of anguish—of how he'd said, "You broke my heart," he let her know how much it hurt when Molly left the Catholic Church. And I, for one, never thought of it like that. All I saw was the shape of his rage. All I saw was meanness.

And Molly, I'm certain, said something about the Great Big Love of the Lord. But she didn't argue and she didn't defend, I don't imagine. I imagine, instead, that Molly prayed, prayed that Yabbo would say every word he needed to say in order to carve his name on heaven's door before he slipped away.

And, I imagine, the words she spoke to Yabbo were something like the things she said to me during my own half-hearted attempt to forgive her. I imagine she told him that she loved him, that she had always loved him, and that he would always be Yabbo to her.

With a voice that sounded too deep, and a throat that sounded too dry, Yabbo, wrapping every syllable in borrowed breath, said something like, "I love you too" before they rested a moment in the silence of their exchange.

And Molly, who saw a missing tooth on the key to heaven, knew just what she was doing when she added, "And Brendan? Do you love Brendan? Do you have anything you want to say to him?"

And with his answer, Yabbo was free.

• • •

The nurse was in the room—she was adjusting his sheet—when he began to make that unmistakable sound. It was the sound that never failed to silence time, never failed to bring all motion to the brink of such stillness that, just then, every nurse within hearing range would stop, tip her head back, and know that she was breathing in.

Like the old woman with the white linen who prepares the table for Communion, Yabbo's nurse took her place in this quiet act of consecration. As two hands came to rest on the ascending warmth of a good, long life, she whispered, "Listen . . . "

And Nonna, who'd never left his side, reached for her husband's hand and closed her eyes.

My mother was sitting at her desk when she received the phone call from my aunt who was standing at her kitchen counter. "It's Dad," she told my mother. "He is taking his last breaths."

• • •

In the years since Yabbo died in peace, I've begun to wonder what it is about reuniting with those by whom we feel most betrayed, what it is—about reconciling— that we allow ourselves to remember as we approach the passage between life and death. What is it—as we prepare to leave the body behind us—that we cannot bear to recall until we begin to die?

And what if we decided not to wait? What if we elected to remember in life? What would happen, at the center of the ordinary life, if the disciplined heart refused to forget?

What would it take?

When Molly reached for her Bible that day, it fell in my hands the way a cellar door, left well ajar, slams shut. A sudden draft in the shape of a chop to the throat and I clammed up tight. For years, that sound would pound on the drums and bounce off the walls inside my heart. Twenty years would roll like thunder before I would open my mouth and speak of it. Nonna herself would lie cold in the casket of a frigid church before I would roll away the stone and stand up straight.

Meanwhile, I would arrange it so that discordant voices among the pro-choice and pro-life—so that clashing forces from the Christian left and the religious right—could not only tell each other stories but hear each other's song, would not only see each other's eyes but listen to each other's sound.

It was only talk. But it would make a Gregorian chant of ringside jeers and referee calls. It was only dialogue. But before long, their arias, their choruses, their orchestras would begin to blend. It was only wind. But it turned a ten-count on the mat into a white baton when the lights went down.

First Be Reconciled

So when you are offering your gift
at the altar, if you remember that your brother
or sister has something against you, leave your gift before
the altar and go; first be reconciled to your brother or
sister, and then come and offer your gift.
—Matthew 5:23–24

What Does Love Look Like?

We are any group of nervous people meeting for the first time. Or maybe not. Gay and straight, Left and Right, we come from churches with blood-letting differences about the Bible and how to use it, about sexuality and how to express it, about the human heart and how to handle it. We range in age from twenty-nine to sixty-two (there are eight of us) we are five women and three men; we are two Asians and six Caucasians; we are three gay people and three evangelicals; we are a lip-biting, hair-twirling, nose-diddling bunch of adversaries but we are sitting face-to-face.

We are not the first group of nervous people to meet in Peace Chapel; we are not the last group of Reconcilers to buck the tide and flip the map. We are three pastors, two students, a therapist, a graphic artist and a lawyer; and we are not the Reconcilers who had a single meeting before the Twin Towers collapsed. We are not the group in which Nora Nash posed a question in such a whisper that nobody heard her. We are the group, a year later, who answered her.

"What does love look like?" she'd asked.

But we are not the group, while the press was serving up scares of anthrax and small pox, who blessed the bread and passed the cup. We are the group whose government has detonated Afghanistan. We are the group whose president, with fabricated "intelligence," will entertain with "shock and awe." As far as we know, we are any group of nervous people whose country has gone to war.

On September 11, 2002, we enter the room for the first time.

On the global field of religious conflict, we know right where we stand. From the Christian Left to the Religious Right, *The Lord our God, the Lord is One* and as far as we know, we are locked in unJesus jihad.

Or maybe not.

Looking around the room, it isn't altogether clear who is gay and who is not, who's on the Right and who's on the Left. A year to the day after an act of hate took three thousand American lives; eight people from opposite poles of the "culture wars" are facing each other in pairs.

Asking our dialogue partners to look back over the year since the Twin Towers fell, we are searching for a quote, a picture or an anecdote; we are reaching for that precious memory, that indelible image of human beings stepping up, of human beings doing things that raise the hand to the heart.

Stop for a moment. What comes to mind?

Imagine you are a native New Yorker. In a city known for its warp-drive and sonic boom—bankers, bikers and short-order cooks are lining the sidewalks in silence. You step out of your van, feel for your gloves, and head past the still life to ground zero. Helmet under your arm, boots up to your knees, the sound of applause—it takes you by surprise—filling your chest until your heart wants to burst. Morning after morning, weeks after the worst was over, rescue workers got that treatment from their fellow native New Yorkers.

Across the continent one year later—reaching down into the bloodiest thing to soak American soil since the Civil War—eight people are handing each other shards of hope. There is something about it; we get off to a good start. We don't pretend nothing bad has happened; and we don't pretend, in the American Church, that nobody is getting hurt.

The Reconcilers

ED MAH

If Ed invites you in for a bowl of soup, the only right answer is Yes. That would be *Yes* to pork shoulder and eggplant potage flavored by anything wrinkling in the vegetable bin; that would be *Yes* to lotus roots in bone marrow broth (don't think; just slurp) and listen to your *chi* sing.

Ed has one of those Chinese faces that grows more and more appealing with age. (The occasional addition of a long goatee does nothing to distract you from thoughts of the *I Ching* or, for that matter, *The Tao of Pooh*.)

At the time of FBR, Ed was celebrating 26 years with his partner, David. Ed, often quiet, is surprisingly articulate about his passionate friendship with Christ. No stranger to Quan Yin and Duplicate Bridge, he is no stranger to sushi, sapphire rings or hand-painted ties.

MARGARET ALTER

Besides being an author, a Marriage and Family Counselor, as well as a professor of Christian Psychology, Margaret—wife, mother and grandmother—has been a teacher, a missionary, a Spiritual Director and an advocate for equality on many fronts.

Voicing great concern about "the addiction to being

right" and how "that didn't seem to go over too well with Jesus," she hopes "to sort out the place of love." Can we "talk this out as churches in conflict?" she asks. "Can we make a model so that bombing Afghanistan doesn't have to happen?"

As a champion of justice and a lover of Scripture, she stands ready to remind us of the power of vulnerability and the call to love. In so doing, Margaret, more than any other participant, is the voice of reconciliation itself.

KAREN STOKES

Karen has been a pastor for over twenty years. She speaks about God as if God grew up next door, as if God built a tree-fort in Karen's backyard. Her confidence clear, her voice the color of a Georgia peach, she isn't preachy; she's generous. When she states her position, she can put up her dukes, but when she talks about Love, she has nothing to prove.

She waxes eloquent about her old boss "who would always look for the human being rather than reduce someone to an issue or a stance." But, she adds, "when you talk about Scripture, it gets scarier."

A Berkeley native, a Northern California liberal, and a Caesar Chavez progressive, she wears a cross and she talks about Jesus like she knows what he likes in his potato salad. The wife of another pastor, a mother of sons and a lover of horses, she is companion to five dogs and six chickens; she is the Senior Pastor to an active congregation that welcomes and blesses gay people and their families.

EDWIN MUNG

By the time he came to First Be Reconciled, Edwin would be in the states for nine years, during which time he would complete his thesis at an evangelical seminary while serving as the Associate Pastor of a conservative Chinese congregation.

"I don't hate you," he needed to tell me, as he served me tea in his church kitchen. "But the Bible, you know, what can I do?" As his four-year-old daughter flashed me a silly smile and wrapped herself around a big leg, her father signed on for dialogue.

Without the combination of Edwin's curiosity and courage, we would have learned a lot less about the conservative perspective, a lot less about the Chinese family, and a lot less about the possibilities of love in the face of national strife and international intolerance.

LISA CASEY

If you can take the girl out of Catholic school but not the Catholic School out of the girl, Lisa walks that middle world where papal roots reach up through the foggy streets of one of the most progressive cities in the U.S.

Like one whose heart is both awakened and broken by the same song, she makes you wonder how the clarion call sounds inside as she thinks out loud and invites you into her interior world. The youngest person in the room, she moves the process along by stepping up to the mound and pitching a story that some might hold back in the "mixed company" of allies and adversaries.

As she speaks in an even voice, her hands at rest on the tabletop, you meet a San Francisco native who has returned to school for a Masters in theology. As she remembers faces and spins yarns about the people and places that have shaped her, you meet a young lesbian who has not run from "difference" but has sought, instead, to engage, be moved, and be transformed by "the enemy."

STEVE BROWN

Steve looks the way some might expect the minister of a Nazarene church to look: the neat short hair; the clean-shaven face; the button-down shirt. If not for the leather bomber jacket and the sports car with the top down, you might be surprised when this evangelical pastor arrives with no Bible under his arm.

Not the sort to redefine love in order to convince himself he's doing it, Steve is the kind of guy who looks into the nature of love and extends love until love is experienced, until love is felt.

Steve, former science teacher, is a man who seeks to learn all he can before he makes up his mind. He's evangelical; he loves the Bible; and he's curious. In his quest to learn about other religions, he engages in interfaith dialogue. In his quest to learn about HIV, he serves lunch to people with AIDS.

When invited to consider First Be Reconciled, he drove an hour up Highway 101 to the café where he signed on as my co-facilitator. He looks at all sides before he makes up his mind, and then he makes up his mind.

BETH RILEY

There was little indication, on day one, that an evangelical from "a quiet charismatic church" was about to endow FBR with a depth of myth and a level of faith that would transform future stories into *heroes' journeys*. But Beth had made a decision to trust this group.

Maybe this trust was the natural scope of one who had said she had come to learn, and in so doing, might change. And maybe, in the course of sharing a dream that had swept ashore like a message in a bottle, she had not only popped the cork but had come to grant our fondest wish.

Beth was the one who spoke of her life in such a way that gay people felt unburdened by gay stereotypes. Beth was the one, pulling threads from mediation to motherhood, who wove the warp and weft in such a way that the Left and Right stood wrapped in the same cloth.

Maybe, in the course of weaving a dream, she had not only made a decision to trust but had fulfilled her hope "to be unafraid of change." In so doing, like the "Magic Helper" in the fairy tales, the genie was out of the bottle. Or maybe the toothpaste was out of the tube. At any rate, she swept awake before our very eyes, and she had us laughing like loons.

PEGGY GREEN

While my own path is eclectic and inclusive, and while my image of Jesus is shaped as much by the *Gnostic Gospels* and *A Course in Miracles* as it was by Catholic School, I believe in the power of a common language. I believe in the language of Love.

Besides First Be Reconciled and similar peacemaking projects, my public journey includes facilitated dialogue between Pro-choice and Pro-life women. My hope for this group is that we will use both spiritual practice and religious faith for everything they're worth. My hope is that all the words I see around forgiveness—I've counted 49 in the New Testament—add up to something tangible.

With the support of Pacific School of Religion and the Graduate Theological Union, my grandest hope for First Be Reconciled, is that it can grandly contribute to the ability of the American church to deal with conflict in a way that is inspiring for the rest of the country.

Where God Is When I Become Who I Am

"Your identity disappears and your ego disappears and you are a part of something magnificent and great and far beyond the sum of its parts."

At a time when four members of Congress are meeting in secret about a program designed to wrench information from the mouths of enemy combatants, eight reconcilers are summoning memories of considerable change, and therefore considerable courage. On a day when a bipartisan committee is treated to a tour of the shattering methods that make prisoners talk, eight people hear the hearts and minds of those they hope to better understand. As elected officials approve the practice of "waterboarding," ordinary people, sharing a moment of silence, are saying the Prayer of St. Francis.

I give you one month to reveal yourself to me.

I was raised in a very fundamentalist environment. My stepmother was a minister in the Salvation Army. And in college, I started to question God. *Is God really real? Or was I just taught this?* I mean, I was taught that this is a floor; I was taught that that is a tree. And was God really real?

I went to a youth rally and talked to a young minister. And he said, "I can't just give you a scripture and you will find God. I can't just tell you to drink this and you will get God. But if you are really questing to find God, God will reveal Himself. *So*," he said, "Challenge God!" And I did. I put God on the line. I said, "Okay, I give you one month . . . to reveal yourself to me."

And one night, I was asleep in my dormitory. And I woke up—it was three in the morning—and every light in my room was lit. I mean, I was woken as if I wasn't asleep. I was wide-awake. And it was warm. I mean, I was in this state where I knew I could just walk out and God would be there. So, at 4 am, I got dressed, walked all over campus, and started to view the creation of God.

He's my father, but sometimes he's like a stranger because, in Chinese culture, we don't talk so much.

When my father was dying, I stayed three days with him in the hospital, and I held his hand. And I realized, "Oh! He's my father but sometimes he's like a stranger," because, in Chinese culture, we don't talk so much.

Even though, I showed my appreciation, like, "Dad, I really appreciate what you have done—your teaching," he said, "Oh, don't mention that; don't mention it."

I'm happy that I tried to express my appreciation and my love to my dad before he died. One of my concerns, of course, is that he did not accept Jesus Christ. But I think I'm not the one to judge him—if he goes to hell or whatever—but I trust God, that He'll do the rest.

LISA

My name is not "I Was."

About six years ago, I started work as an elementary school teacher. And along with it, came a lot of insomnia and bodily stress. Illness. Every night, I would collapse. Like I would fall asleep but then, around two in the morning, I'd wake up and think of everything I'd done wrong that day and all the things I was afraid of the next day. It was like a year of that.

When I left teaching, I went up to Maine, and was living in a little religious community, sort of. I saw this book called *I Am*. I opened it up and it said, "When you live in the past, with its regrets and disappointments, life is hard because my name is not 'I Was.' But when you live in the future, with all its uncertainties and fears, life is hard because my name is not 'I Will Be.'"

It was one of those times—more than many scriptures because I've been inundated with that my whole life—when I just felt like that was God's Word. That was God talking, saying, "This is the work you will need to do in order to live."

BETH

I felt this huge rush of spiritual energy, coming down through the top of my head.

It was my very first mediation training. The instructor set up a fishbowl exercise where everybody else was sitting in a circle, and I was on the inside, in a chair. He asked me to explain why I wanted to do mediation.

I took a breath, and was getting ready to deliver my answer when I felt this huge rush of spiritual energy, coming down through the top of my head, filling my whole body. It was a completely, loving, peaceful energy. It matched this motivation I had to be a peacemaker, to do something in connection with what God would have me do.

But my ego was kind of off in the distance, up on a shelf. I was totally focused on reconciliation and cooperation.

KAREN

The singers disappeared and we all became this one
great voice.

I was in college, in the choir, rehearsing for a concert
that night. We were all on stage in this huge empty hall
when it happened: the singers disappeared and we all
became this one great voice.

We were singing the one-hundred-and-twenty-
somethingth psalm, where "those who sow in tears will
reap in joy," and we just became that text and everyone
felt it. There was this unity of experience where your
identity disappears and your ego disappears, and you
are a part of something magnificent and great and far
beyond the sum of its parts.

And that's where I experienced God—in that dis-
solution of ego where you get to disappear and the
Spirit inhabits the whole experience.

MARGARET

Taking that as a nudge from God, I called my sister.

My older sister and I have never gotten on very well.

I'm an extrovert; she's an introvert; something would happen that was really special and she would wait her time to tell it. But, you know, I was the little sister, proud of her, and I would blurt out her story before she had a chance to tell it. She wanted to kill me.

So I said to God, "You're the God of reconciliation. You like to do hard things. The ball's in your court." Some interesting things happened. I started working with the Myers-Briggs test as a career counselor. The test shows how important differences are and how misunderstanding can happen. So, taking that as a nudge from God, I called my sister. And sure enough, we are opposites on three poles.

She and I have quite a nice relationship now. And I think it's just that "something" that happens that is God, that I can trust. It's sort of like, "Show up if you are really God." I can say, "This is yours; I don't know how to do it."

Stereotypes, Pigeonholes and Positive Disappointments

"I realized there was diversity in the group, a group I had pigeonholed as being all the same. But they weren't all the same."

*He had a pretty blonde wife and four cute blonde sons
and the whole thing.*

I was working on my doctorate a few years ago. There
was a small group of us, all working pastors; it was a
very diverse group: a couple of African-American pastors, me, a young woman from Japan, a guy from Aus-
tralia, and one young, white, evangelical, male pastor
from Los Angeles. And that fits a lot of stereotypes.
And he had a pretty blonde wife and four cute blonde
sons and the whole thing.

He had just done a $40 million project that added
a school to his church, and I just thought that this guy
was really out of touch.

One Sunday, he went to San Francisco to go to Glide
Memorial Church. There's a large gay constituency in
that church, and he got to talking with some gay Christians. He came back to class the next day and said, "If I
discovered that one of my sons was gay, I would want
to know that there was a church that would welcome
him."

And it was so open of him to say that. He made
himself so vulnerable. Because he had built his life on
a different set of assumptions. What allowed that to
happen? We had reached a level of trusting and know-

ing each other as individuals. It made him feel that he didn't have to defend some point of view to us. It made us feel that we didn't have to keep him out there as that Straight, White, Male.

EDWIN

If you go to church, don't come back home; just stay in the church.

I was around 14 years old and living in Hong Kong, when I accepted Jesus Christ as my Lord and Savior. But when I got back home, and told my mom, it was a big conflict because my mom was worshiping our ancestor. So, I was really confused. But I sensed the presence of God. But my mom was strongly against me. You know, "If you go to church, don't come back home; just stay in the church."

So I didn't know what to do. Should I be faithful to my understanding of God? Do I have to surrender that? Or should I try to preserve my relationship with my mom? It was really tough but I stayed home and worshiped in another way.

LISA

I wanted to do it so badly that I resolved that I wasn't going to come out.

I had a positive disappointment. I was living in New Jersey, and when I got ready to leave there, I decided I was gonna' go to this community in Maine where they engage in theological study and build boats! I said, "I want to do that!" But I had no idea where they stood on gay stuff. And Bobby, who ran the place, was a minister in the United Church of Christ. And I had never heard of this denomination.

But I wanted to do the other stuff so badly that I resolved that I wasn't going to come out because I really wanted to work on wooden boats, and I really wanted scholastic exposure to the Bible.

I had just spent two years teaching where my whole life was "Don't ask; Don't tell," and it was the first time in my whole life when it was like that.

But I said, "I'm going to Maine!" So in a day or two of arriving, Ruth, who is married to Bobby, pulls out her rainbow sticker that says, "Straight But Not Narrow" and starts dropping little hints.

BETH

They always had more depth and more spirit than I wanted to give them credit for.

From the time I started attending this church back in 1978, I picked up on the fact that our little church was at loggerheads with the umbrella organization. Twenty-five years later, the umbrella organization rewrote the theological statement and our church wasn't prepared to accept it.

So I ended up being the representative from our church, going to a lot of meetings. But what I found was that every time I went, things would always happen so that I couldn't put them in a box. They always had more depth and more spirit, than I wanted to give them credit for.

We were arguing about capital punishment when I stood up. And then other people stood up. They said these really prophetic things. And I realized there was diversity in the group, a group that I had pigeonholed as being all the same. But they weren't all the same.

KAREN

In the North, she kept being taken up short because racism was much more subtle.

When I first started college in 1970, one of the other women at the college was African-American. And she was talking about how difficult it was to be black in the North. As opposed to in the South where racism is fairly right out there. She said, in the North, she kept being taken up short because racism is much more subtle; because people sound like they're being affirming of you, and then all of a sudden you know that the line just got drawn.

MARGARET

I always think of the Good Samaritan, the last person you expect to stop and help you."

In our church, some years back, there was a lot of talk about how evangelicals are this, that, and the other thing. A lot of stereotypes. And then I got hired to teach at an evangelical center, New College. And I went in with some excitement but also with some degree of anxiety about conservatives. So I went to chapel to connect with the community. And there I was, standing next to one of my evangelical colleagues, singing. And she sang Inclusive Language[5] straight through every hymn. I always think of the Good Samaritan: the last person you expect to stop and help you.

Hurtful and Healing
Uses of Scripture

*"When I was fourteen, my father committed
suicide. I'd never been to church before
and I wondered if he was damned."*

For the first four sessions—between the weeks when Eddie "Gwen" Araujo[6] was last seen at a Newark party and three young men were charged with "hate-crime enhanced" murder—Steve and I ran the show, all along training the others to take over our role. As Steve and I join the discussion, the others begin pairing off, each pair consisting of two from opposing points of view. Going straight for the big-ticket issues, they ask first, for a "hurtful," and second, for a "healing" encounter with the Bible.

BETH

This guy thought that, as a lawyer, I was profiting off of sin.

We had a pastor who decided to preach on the subject of divorce. And he told the story about his brother getting a divorce. But he wrapped up his sermon with the passage that says that unless there is adultery, it's sinful for people to get divorced. End of discussion. That's what Jesus said. And I'm a divorce lawyer.

And it was hurtful to me because somebody who I would've liked to be in harmony with was reading the Bible in a way I disagreed with; it was too simplistic. It was also hurtful that he was up on the pulpit. It was just hurtful that this guy thought that, as a lawyer, I was profiting off of sin.

I'd been thinking about this issue since the day I'd initially read that Scripture when I was 25 years old, before which I was a Unitarian. (And then I was a Marxist.)

What made healing possible was that I'd realized the Bible was really important to me, very authoritative to me. But in my tradition, there is an emphasis on a personal relationship with Christ that enlightens your reading of Scripture. I didn't feel like I had to lay down my law practice.

KAREN

There was this silence on the other end. And I'm thinking, "Here it comes."

When I was first ordained, my husband and I were co-pastors at a church up in Humboldt County. And there were a lot of people who'd come through on Highway 101 who needed a place to stay or food or something.

And I was working in the office one day when the phone rang. And there was a man on the other end who asked me if he could speak to the pastor. And I said, "I am the pastor." And there was this silence on the other end. And I'm thinking, *Here it comes.*

I had had a lot of conversations already, with people who acted like they wanted to discuss with me whether it was alright for women to be ordained. And as I tried to enter into dialogue, what I discovered was that there was no desire for dialogue at all.

So this guy said he was coming through town and he needed a place to stay. So I did the phone calling, and I lined up some food for him, and I lined up a place for him, and he called back, and I told him how to get to the house.

And we were sort of wrapping up all the business, and he said, "Can I ask you a question? How is it that you can be a minister when it says in First Corinthians—"

And I thought, *I really don't wanna go into this again.* So I said, "Okay, if you want to discuss it, we'll discuss it. But what I've found is that usually that's not very fruitful. So what I'm going to say is: "If you don't think God called me to the Ministry, then you don't have to accept this place to stay tonight. But if you do accept this place to stay, then you are admitting that God called me to this work." And he said, "I'll take the place" and he hung up the phone.

And it was like, how many times do you take that?

And I felt kind of bad about forcing him to sort of compromise his ideals in order to take the place to sleep but I also felt like that wasn't really my problem anymore.

And so, what allowed me to reach the place of healing was being clear that God did call me to this, and balancing the responsibility for that guy's opinion back to him. I let him deal with it. I didn't have to take it in again.

And what allowed me to heal was that for several years I was already doing the work that God had called me to do. I was preaching. I was counseling people. I was doing the stuff that I felt God had enabled me to do.

And so getting clearer and clearer that I am an ordained minister in the church of Jesus Christ made it possible for me to not take his invalidating of me as personally as I had been taking it in the past.

And what was it about me that made the healing possible? Just that I wanna be faithful to God, and I want to be faithful to other people, and I thought that the most loving thing to do for him in that moment was to not take that crap from him.

Allender:

let them feel the
weight of who
you are ...

I kept telling myself, "Hey, I'm an all right person."

I used to be a member of this big men's group. And my team leader wanted me to attend a conference that we were putting together, and I had a conflict: my sister was up from San Diego. I had made some plans to spend the weekend with her. And this guy really read me the riot act. He quoted all these Scriptures, "Seek ye first the kingdom of God," and all this stuff, terrible stuff.

I was actually in tears because I felt terrible about all the stuff he was saying to me. But I told him, "No, this is what I'm doing."

And although I felt terrible at the time, I think what made the healing possible was the fact that I kept telling myself, "Hey, I'm an all right person. This is not going to affect my life the way this guy says it will." And it really was a turning point for me, in terms of my relationship with the group. What he was saying to me hurt me so much that it allowed me to reflect upon balance and all the other priorities in my life: my family, my schoolwork.

So what made the healing possible was the ability to reflect, to put it in perspective, confirming within myself that I was okay.

EDWIN

I got a lot of criticism from a lot of people. Like, "Being a pastor, you're so mean."

A few years ago, when I had a conflict with a member of the church, I tried to keep it private. I didn't want to reveal the problem to the whole congregation.

But this fellow, he was really self-centered. He was on a lot of committees and gave the church a lot of money but it seemed to me that he liked to do whatever he wanted. If he didn't like the color we'd chosen, he'd go buy a five-gallon can and paint the sanctuary green. I tried to confront him about it. But I got a lot of criticism from a lot of people like, "Being a pastor, you're so mean. You are not loving to this person." It hurt me for a while.

In the very beginning, I was a little bit self-righteous. Later on, I thought I should have had more patience, and given him more chances. Maybe my words had hurt him.

And finally I said to myself, "It's God who's going to judge me. Not other people." And I realized that I'm not perfect. I'm never going to be perfect, and I will hurt other people.

She is standing just inside the bedroom we used to share when she turns, lifts the Bible up off the bed and places it in my hand.

When I was 21, my sister was 24, and that was the year that I came out as a lesbian and she came out as a born-again Christian. I'm sure that was a great year for my mom.

One day, when my sister and I were both at my mom and dad's, my sister called me up the stairs and I sprinted up to see what she wanted. She is standing just inside the doorway to the bedroom we used to share, when she turns, lifts the Bible up off the bed and places it in my hand. And she puts her finger—I'll never forget it—right there. Romans,chapter 1, verse 26.[7]

And that was my introduction to the Bible. It was like, *Thanks so much! I'll read more of this!*

I just published an article about a recent conversation I had with my sister about that moment. And she didn't remember handing me that Bible at all. It completely sets the course of my life and she has no memory of it.

It was six o'clock in the morning, and my mother was sitting waiting for me. And she said, "Where have you been?"

Well, this really hits home. I had a stepmother who was a minister in the Salvation Army. And she raised us kids. And when I was in high school—this was back in Idaho—and there weren't many gay people or gay places in Idaho.

And so sometimes, after working until two o'clock in the morning in our restaurant, I would walk the streets and hope someone would pick me up. And we'd have some time and then I would go home.

And one time I came home, it was six o'clock in the morning, and my mother was sitting and waiting for me. And she said, "Where have you been?" "Oh, just walking around."

And then she asked me if I was gay. And I said no. And she started giving me this lecture, and finally I admitted I was gay, and she told me to read Leviticus.[8]

And I read it, and she said, "What does that mean to you?" It meant that I was going to hell. Because this was an abomination. And I ended up saying to her, "If I am going to hell, at least I'm going to be with people that love me."

Well she freaked out. She started crying. And she kept saying, "You don't know how much I love you." So anyway, we kind of parted ways. I soon went to college and didn't spend a lot of time at home.

And while I was in school, I realized that what she did was very hurtful to me at the time; but she did things out of love. She wasn't trying to be mean. And she did all of these things with the abilities that she had. And that was what she knew. So I realized that she loved me.

And she has passed away. And at the funeral, a friend of ours came to me and said, "I'm really glad your mother and you had a reconciliation." And I looked at her, "Really? When was this?"

And she said, "Well, your mother talked to me and said that she really understood and things were okay."

And I felt good.

The Bible wasn't solely that one bad experience that I remember most.

When I first started at Pacific School of Religion, I was looking for a good course in New Testament. And I could have taken it from any one of the famous feminist scholars at the Graduate Theological Union. But after 30 years, I didn't need anyone to tell me how to be a feminist anymore. I wanted to take the course from somebody whose most stellar qualification was that she, or he, just *loved the book.* So I asked around and everyone said, "Bob Smith."

And I have to say that what was healing was his teaching style. Because it enabled me to go into it from a place of enthusiasm. I didn't walk in there with this big bag of bad memories. He'd just ask this fabulous question—and take five paces back. And the whole class would go, "Boom!"

Does anyone remember that TV show, "Welcome Back, Kotter?"[9] Well, I was that kid with the hand in the air, going, "Ooh-Ooh-Ooh!"[10]

What made healing possible? Being open to the fact that there might be something good in the Bible, that the Bible wasn't solely that one bad experience I remember most.

*This attitude towards women was something I was
going to have to deal with before I got any further.*

I was still in law school when I began reading the Bible
and encountering these treasured verses in First Corinthians[11] and First Timothy[12] about silence as the pre-
ferred state for women.

I realized that this attitude towards women (as
unequal) was something that I was going to have to
deal with before I got any further. And if I didn't find
some way, I was gonna' have trouble with Christianity.

So I went out and read some books that were written by women—I still have them—I needed to know
that there were other Christians who were intelligent,
and who had thought about it, and who were very
faithful. Because I considered myself the equal of a
man. And if the Bible wasn't going to let me continue
with that belief, then I was going to walk away from it.

But I was so drawn to this Bible . . .

Okay, am I willing to die on the cross?

The most conflicting passage of the Bible for me is Jesus' example as a pastor. I had to ask myself whether I was willing to sacrifice, sometimes my dignity or maybe my life, to love my congregation. We can go back to the same incident of the conflict with the fellow on all the church committees.

It was around Easter time when a group of people came to me to tell me to apologize to him and to do whatever he wanted. It split the church; they wanted to leave the church. And I was in a big struggle. And so I did apologize. Not because of fear and the loss of so many people. But because, "Okay, am I willing to die on the cross? Just like Christ?" That was my feeling at the time.

If our motive is not love then it's not right.

I grew up in a church where there was a lot of Scripture used to keep people's sins at bay. There were a lot of do's and don'ts. There was no going to see movies; no alcohol; no cigarettes; no dancing. So, I came out of that.

And just after I graduated from denominational college, I heard a series of messages by a theologian who talked about John Wesley. And one of the things that Wesley said was, "God's nature and his name is Love." Love is what God is at the core.

And regardless of whether or not we do all the things we are supposed to do and are supposed to avoid doing, if our motive is *not* love, then it's *not* right. It was a liberating moment. I connected a lot of biblical dots. The evidence of God in my life is love.

KAREN

I went to his funeral really frightened of what was going to be said in Church about a man who'd committed suicide.

My father was a divorce lawyer. We weren't raised in the church at all. My father thought the church was filled with hypocrites, people that he dealt with all week long and didn't want to sit next to in church. But he was very devoted to justice, and he volunteered in Legal Aid, protecting Mexican migrant workers from their landlords.

When I was 14, he committed suicide. I'd never been to church before, and I knew that suicide wasn't very acceptable in the church, and I wondered if he was damned. The funeral was going to be in a Presbyterian church, because the pastor there was a good friend of my father's, and they had worked together on a number of social justice projects.

But the pastor my dad knew was on vacation—it was August—so I went into this funeral really frightened of what was going to be said in the Christian Church about a man who'd committed suicide. In the midst of all this other trauma, I was sitting there wondering if lightning was gonna come down through the roof.

The Education Minister ran the service. And when he gave the homily, he read from Matthew 25: "Come, you blessed of my Father, and receive your reward . . . *for I was hungry and you gave me food, I was thirsty and you gave me drink.*" And it—it saved my life.[13]

Sexual Identity and Other Discoveries

"In Chinese culture, you have this great wall. You don't talk about things. So I never told my father I was gay."

While young men pack their vests and belts with the nuts and bolts that will sear the flesh from 183 tourists in Bali, a Chinese American and a Chinese immigrant—a gay Catholic and an evangelical pastor—lead eight people to articulate the intimate discoveries that become a turning point for the entire group.

KAREN

Maybe gender identity was just what you had—for the duration.

I grew up in a family of brothers; I'm the one girl. Two brothers were older and two were younger. I remember when I was a little girl, maybe five or six, I just assumed that everybody got to be both, that my brothers were girls for a while and then, at some point, they got to be boys; and that I was a girl and at some at some point, I would get to be a boy. So I said, "When I'm a little boy—" and my brothers roared with laughter. And I was so stunned. It was the first inkling I had that maybe gender identity was just what you had— for the duration.

My brothers and I were always critiquing each other by what we laughed at. But there was always that sense that I wasn't going to limit what I was going to do based on whether I was laughed at. And then one of my brothers, William, ended up being gay.

But just a few years ago, when I was driving to church, I heard a song by Dar Williams,[14] about how she would ride her bike and climb trees and drive her mother crazy with the risks she would take. And how society redefined that for her. "But," she sings, "I will not forget that I was a boy."[15] And in the last verse, she's talking to a male friend to whom she says that she has lost and the men have won, and they have forced her into this role. And he says, "No. When I was a girl, I used to pick flowers with my mother, and I could cry when I needed to." And I burst into tears; I had to pull over and collect myself.

STEVE

I remember withdrawing my arm—like, "Whoa!"

I was a late bloomer. I didn't start dating girls until I was in college. I was very close to a friend throughout my high school years, a guy who came to our church. We were very close; we spent a lot of time together, mostly because his mother was struggling with cancer. She eventually died when we were juniors in high school.

And I remember, when we walked home from school—this was in the late 60s, early 70s—we'd walk home with our arms around each other's shoulders. Like this. It was a natural thing for us to do. And I remember the time—I don't know what happened—but suddenly, I realized—I remember withdrawing my arm—like, *Whoa!*

But it was part of the friendship, just putting our arms around each other and being good buddies. But we never did it again.

That was the first time I knew I was a boy.

I was the oldest in the family, and my sister was six years younger when I realized my sexual identity. I was in kindergarten and we tried to play the doctor and patient game when I realized, "Oh! We are different!"

We weren't really naked but we tried to find out, "Hey, what's wrong with your body?" And that was the first time I knew that I was a boy. And that I was different from a girl.

But culturally speaking, it was not just physical. Your character, your way of behaving, had to be different from that of a girl.

It was not such a big deal when I was young but when I grew up, I was a social worker in Hong Kong when I found out that they don't expect you to be compassionate, to show your emotions. That to me is hard. I tend to be more feminine. Even though I'm pretty sure I'm a man!

LISA

She had assumed that I'd been sexually abused and that living as a gay person was the best I could do.

I came out when I was 19, in the summer between my first and second years of college. While I was a student, I volunteered as a trainer in the athletics department. I would tape ankles and run the machines. I wound up being a manager for the women's basketball team. So I would hang out at practice every day.

And there was a writer—she wrote Christian books— who had befriended several of the players on the team. So, I'd be at practice with the video camera, and she, Rhonda would be there watching her friends, and we just got to know each other. And I told her I'd just come out—I wasn't going to hide it.

One day, I realized from some of her questions that there was this picture she had of my life. She had assumed that I had been sexually abused, that I was in a constant state of recovery, and that living as a gay person was the best that I could do to cope with the violence that had been done to me by men. And I was just shocked. She had created this entire identity for me.

God was in my understanding that my sexuality was a gift; it was a gift from God. It wasn't a patch.

MARGARET

The role of women was so constrained and confined, very repressive and proper and horrible.

One of my earliest memories is of my older sister chasing me around the backyard with a pair of underpants. So I presume I was naked. And along with that, was her kind of tut-tut, bossy older sister attitude. I was in the middle of three girls.

And my mother was very proper and came from a very proper British family with all the right ways of doing things, which I never did. I was a very bold child. And I guess my saving grace was my dad. He really liked the boldness. He liked the fact that I was outspoken.

And when he came back from World War II, he wanted to do something for us girls and we wanted to ride. So we had riding lessons. And I think that really saved me. Because you can be really aggressive and bold on a horse. And I think God was in the boldness because I was determined that I was going to have another life besides 'housewife.'

The role of women was so constrained and confined, very repressive and proper and horrible. It was terrifying to me.

Being the only Asian in my class, I was very inward always. But I was always experimenting, trying to find this gayness.

I'm from Idaho. And growing up there, where my mother had passed away, I had a stepmother and my Chinese father.

I never knew my father growing up at all. Because he would go to work at three o'clock in the afternoon and come home maybe three in the morning. And so I would never see my father until the weekends.

I knew in high school, maybe even in middle school, that I had more interest in males than females. And I was also kind of shy in high school. Being the only Asian in my class, I was very inward always. But I was always experimenting, trying to find this gayness.

My stepmother was a very fundamentalist Christian, and the only thing I knew about gay things was that they were bad. It was not a good thing to have all these feelings about. And so I just kept all these things hidden inside. Until the time when my stepmother confronted me, and it all came out.

But then I realized that I could love Christ almost as a lover, and that he could love me back almost as a lover. We had that relationship. And I could accept my own Christianity and my own gayness. And so as an adult, I feel very fortunate that I have a partner, David. And Christ is like an unjealous lover, and He gives me a bonus in life. And my bonus is David. I feel very comfortable being gay.

But my father, we never talked about it. In Chinese culture, you have this great wall. You don't talk about things. And so I never told my father I was gay. And whenever I saw him, he would say, "Oh, you should get married." Even when I was forty-eight. It wasn't wrong to be gay. But you need to have a family. And so my father passed away and we never, ever talked about it.

BETH

There were people running around, banging on the
windows and it was something dreadful.

Um, this is pretty personal for me. The thing that came
to mind was a dream. As I was listening to everybody
else talk, I realized that this is not only a dream about
sexual identity; it's a defining moment. It's a dream
where I became reconciled—to my sexual identity,
which I hadn't accepted.

The dream occurred when I was 22. I didn't menstruate when the other girls did. I got into dieting when
I was about 14. When I was 15, I was anorexic.

From age 15 or 16, I was absolutely certain—I was
determined to live my life single. I would never get
married.

A few years later, I went through a really promis-
cuous period that lasted about four years. Towards
the end of it, I was in college, taking Women's Studies
courses in a school that was mostly women, where I
had a number of lesbian friends and acquaintances.

I had a couple of very brief lesbian relationships—
and discovered that I wasn't physically attracted to
women. And I had previous knowledge that I was
attracted to men. And this was something of a disappointment actually. I was not disinclined to be rid of
men.

Anyway, I had a dream. And in this dream—a very symbolic, kind of Hitchcockian dream—I was in a suburban house and it was dark and there was no furniture. And there were people running around, banging on the windows, and it was something dreadful; I had some kind of horrible feeling. But anyway, I went into the fireplace and dug. And I unearthed this buried, decomposing baby. And this was such a startling moment, I woke up.

The following morning, I felt this extremely sharp pain in my abdomen that just doubled me over. That evening, I started to menstruate.

Within a year or so, I realized that I did want to reproduce and have a family. I realized I actually wanted to have children in my life—which was another indication that I was going to have to deal with men. But I became reconciled, at that point, to my female sexuality. I think, after that, I really embraced it.

Sex in the Bible

"When I ran into Lot going to bed with his daughters, I was too embarrassed to ask what that was about."

This morning, the Reconcilers pursue a closer understanding of the places where we part company. Today, as we approach one of the colder fronts in the Culture Wars, our responses stray from structured dialogue to open conversation. Today, as we both uphold and challenge the authority of the Bible, we lay bare the many "authorities" to which each of us turns in times of search.

PEGGY

This is no longer a deity who is wearing the name of the slavemaster's God.

When I think of sexual ethics in the Bible—where men take many wives, where female slaves are used to produce heirs—I think of the story of Hagar who was considered a third-class citizen. Because she was a slave, because she was a foreigner, because she was a woman. And so all of these ethics come into play, as this "slave girl" becomes a sex slave, after which she is cast out into the desert by her owner.

At that point where Hagar is wandering through the desert carrying her infant son and an empty skin of water; at that point where she has no more bread; at that point where her child will surely starve, she enters into conversation with God. And I don't remember how the conversation began but she "puts the boy away from her" because she can't watch him die. At that point, Hagar, a slave, a woman, understands that she has truly been seen by God. And after that, she gives God the name, "El Roi" or "The God Who Sees".[16]

So this is no longer a deity who is wearing the name of the slavemaster's God.

Hagar develops a completely different relationship

with a whole new God. And shortly thereafter—the story that is barely told in the Bible—her son grows up and becomes the founder of a new nation. Today's Islam.

The Bible is a minefield when it comes to sexual behavior.

The Bible plays a huge role in my life. What frames the shape the Bible takes, for me, is table fellowship—the incredible, welcoming, and non-judging behavior of Jesus.

You know, the Bible is a minefield when it comes to sexual behavior. I was sixteen when I first got involved with the church. And when I ran into Lot going to bed with his daughters,[17] I was too embarrassed to ask anyone what that was about.

Another time, I just sort of wandered into Judges 19, "The Levite's concubine,"[18] which is a horrific, horrible story. It takes place in Sodom and Gomorrah. He throws her out to a bunch of men—to be gang-raped all night long. And then they find her in the morning, after she has crawled to the doorstep. Just a horrifying story. The way the story is framed, it's as if the offense committed was not against the woman but against the property of a man.

So, what *is* the view of sex in the Bible? Because, if we lived by the Bible, we'd say that the women are the property of the men, and that men can have lots of wives, and lots of concubines, like Hagar. And so, when someone is taking the Bible literally, I don't know quite how that works. I think it's really frightening, the sexual ethics in the Bible.

EDWIN

I'm not going to use the Bible to condemn people. My understanding is that God is going to do the final judgment.

The Bible plays a really important role in my life. But I keep reflecting on my understanding of the Bible because I think it's not static; I think it's very dynamic. As I grow older and older, or maybe because I have more experience, I have a different understanding of the same passage in the Bible. Even though I'm reading the same passage, the same story, I have a new insight every time.

So I don't use the Bible as a set of rules and regulations, but more as a guideline. And sometimes I have to admit my misunderstanding of the Bible. I have to say, "I'm wrong!"

I'm not going to use the Bible to condemn people. My understanding is that God is going to do the final judgment; I'm not going to. When Jesus sent out his disciples he commanded them to just keep blessing, rather than curse. But if they don't receive the blessing, you just—you move on.[19] And I think that's my attitude.

Christ was saying to love yourself and to love your neighbor.

I heard a priest say, "I really don't care what you do in bed, but I do care how you vote." Regarding morals and ethics, I go to the simple passage, "Love your neighbor as yourself."[20] For me, I can use just that in terms of how I will conduct myself. People like to put everything in black and white: This is right and that's wrong. Regarding things you do sexually that may be hindering to another person or self-gaining for you, or any sex that isn't done in a loving spirit, to me, Christ was saying to love yourself and to love your neighbor, in all of the things you do.

KAREN

I don't want to just go in there to find the things that
already back up what I already believe. I want to be
challenged by it. I want that Spirit to break in.

I told you the story about my father's funeral where
the preacher gave me that life-saving word. So, I think
I went into the Bible expecting to love it. And there are
things in there that frustrate me and infuriate me but,
in general, I have come to embrace it as something that
is central in my life.

I remember grappling with how to decide what
in the Bible is life-giving and what to let slide. And I
heard a researcher say, "I try not to use statistics the
way a drunk uses a lamp post: more for support than
for illumination." And I thought, "I want to have that
attitude towards the Bible." I don't want to just go in
there to find the things that already back up what I
already believe. I want to be challenged by it. I want to
be illuminated. I want that Spirit to break in.

STEVE

Well, what really happened? It opened my eyes to the fact that Scripture can have contradictions.

I grew up in a church that revered the Bible, almost worshiped the Bible. My father put together a parallel of the accounts of Jesus' resurrection. He took all the Gospels and put them all together into one big story. And I remember seeing—I was in high school at the time—that one account says that the angels are sitting on this stone, and another account says that they are inside, and another account says that they look like shepherds or gardeners, out tending the field. So I was thinking, "Well, what really happened?"

It sort of opened my eyes to the fact that Scripture can have contradictions, and that those actually do exist in Scripture. This was an amazing revelation to me.

And in terms of the Scriptures about homosexuality, I was really interested to read *Christianity, Homosexuality and Social Tolerance* by John Boswell.[21] He wrote about the story of Sodom and Gomorrah.[22]

The text says that all the men of the city came to the house. So, are we saying that all of these men wanted to have sex with these strangers that came to town? That doesn't make a whole lot of sense that everyone in the city would be gay.

Then Boswell talks about the Hebrew form of the verb "to know," and that 90% of the time, it simply means "to know." And he talked about the custom of hospitality, that when strangers come to town, it was expected that they would meet with the elders. And they would stay in the "hospitality house" for visitors instead of going off to stay with Lot, this newcomer. So naturally, the elders of the city were outraged.

Boswell talked about the many different Scriptures that referred to Sodom and Gomorrah, and how they didn't talk about homosexuality.

The one reference that Jesus has, to the "sin" of Sodom and Gomorrah, comes as he is sending out his disciples, including to places where they won't be received; places where they are to shake the dust off their sandals because the people will be inhospitable. Jesus compares these people to the people of Sodom and Gomorrah. So the sin of Sodom and Gomorrah, to Jesus, is the sin of inhospitality, which is a huge sin back in those days.[23]

In my denomination, sexual things were not talked about at all. There was one interpretation, which I'd heard maybe once, about the story of Sodom and Gomorrah. But John Boswell allowed me to see that there are other ways of interpreting some of the Scriptures. It was a real revelation to me.

EDWIN

My professor cautioned me not to make this a case that approves this very-close-to-abusive behavior.

My Master's thesis was on the book of Hosea. It's a very fascinating and interesting book about Hosea's wife, Gomer. Hosea tried to discipline—I used the word "discipline"—his wife in certain ways.[24]

But my professor cautioned me not to make this a case that approves this very-close-to-abusive behavior. It's very abusive. The conversation with my professor gave me sensitivity. "Always, from a male perspective and a female perspective," he said, "look at the same story."

BETH

My way of figuring out who I was — was to go as far
as I could go without totally endangering my life. So,
freedom and containment, and how does God want us to
deal with it?

Almost ten years ago, an old friend of mine, who was
in a very vulnerable place, started getting Christian
counseling with a male friend of mine. Well, they got
into an affair. She got totally involved with him; he
broke off the relationship; she was totally devastated
and ended up suing him. I knew many people who
knew them both, and it split us all apart.

But it started me thinking about boundaries for
containing sexual behavior. I went through a period of
my life where I was somewhat out of control. I didn't
know my own boundaries. My way of figuring out
who I was—was to just go as far as I could go without
totally endangering my life. So, freedom and containment, and how does God want us to deal with it?

The attitude of people in my church is that the relationship between you and God is a one-on-one thing.
And the role of the Bible is illumination to the individ-
ual; and the Spirit is speaking to you through the Scripture. And the Spirit can speak to you in other ways,

not just through Scripture. And so, if you are getting anything out of the Bible, it's not because somebody else is telling you what it means. But because you are receiving some truth that is relevant to you.

KAREN

The Bible has authority for me, but it's one of many voices.

I was working on a wedding with a rabbi one time—it was a Jewish and Christian couple—and we decided to meet for a couple of months before the wedding, just to learn about each other's faith traditions. And I said something that kind of assumed the authority of Scripture, and she said, "Well, it's not quite like that for Jews."

She said, "There's a story about a rabbi who has a meeting with the governing board of the congregation. And he's got one point of view, and the people on the board have another point of view, and finally they dismiss him so that they can take a vote. And they call him back in and say, 'Thank you for your input, Rabbi, but the vote was twelve to nothing.' And this voice comes down from heaven and says, 'You should listen to the rabbi; he's a brilliant man.' And the president of the congregation, says, 'Well, make that twelve to one.'"

So the Bible has authority for me but it's one of many voices. And I guess my real relationship with it, is that I love it. And I want to be faithful to that relationship.

LISA

I compare the authority of the words in the Bible to the authority of my own heart.

I was at a speaking engagement in Maine, on a panel of speakers who were either gay or lesbian or a parent of someone who was gay. There isn't a large gay population there. So people are curious; it's not like they see gay stuff integrated into daily life.

So there we were on the panel. And there was a fellow in the audience there who was asking the question, "I'm listening, I see that you are wonderful people, but I'm just sort of struggling because I see in the Scriptures that this is wrong. And I'm just trying to get some help in understanding that." And every speaker there just blew him off. Like, "We're not getting into theological discussions here."

So he pressed them. He said, "No, I'm not trying to antagonize you. Please, could you just tell me about your experience maybe." And they still just brushed him off. And I was so angry at these folks that I wound up getting up and making a scene, and scolding the panelists, and talking to him directly, in a room of 50 or 60 people.

And I told him that, for me, there are Scriptures, there are interpretations, there are different people deciding what's right and wrong, but it really comes down to what's in my heart. And that's where God is.

So I compare the authority of the words in the Bible—I just sit with it—to the authority of my own heart—asking myself in my heart, *Is this okay?* And only coming to one conclusion, and that's that it *is* okay. And I don't know how to reconcile that with different Scriptures, and I don't know how to reconcile that with different people, I don't know how to do all that. I only know how to do what's inside.

And I sensed that he was struggling with the same thing, that his heart was telling him one thing, and his religious surroundings were telling him another thing. And it was a really wonderful moment. It was transforming for me. Like, "Oh, I can't believe I just got up in front of all these people." And I am like in tears with this man who is also in tears.

"Love the Sinner, Hate the Sin"

"I get really upset when people
try to rank sins. Because if homosexuality
is a sin, it's certainly no more sinful than
anything that I am doing."

Today, as we take clear stands and sometimes take surprising ones—as some begin to clarify what they have come to understand, and some are moved by the depth of understanding—we tell stories of a "love" that ranges from the caring to the unkind.

People would post messages saying there is no such thing as a gay Christian, that the two are mutually exclusive.

The first time I heard the "Love the sinner; hate the sin" phrase applied to gay people, it was when I first started learning about the Internet. I stumbled into this discussion group, called something like "Gay and Christian." And it was mostly just gay Christians supporting each other. But anyone could come in and post their thoughts.

So a lot of people would post messages that were very critical of gay people, saying that there is no such thing as a gay Christian and that the two are mutually exclusive.

And there was one person in particular, he was very articulate, and logical, and extremely critical of gay people. And he used that 'love the sinner; hate the sin' line.

You sort of get to know the people who write for these boards. And a number of people who I had come to experience as very thoughtful and faithful would say, "This has to do with our identity; it has to do with how we were created by God and how we are accepted and loved by God."

And that was new to me. To have a gay Christian

saying, "Who I am is not a sinner," really moved me to a new understanding of what it is to be challenged and negated in terms of something that's basic to one's own identity.

And shortly after that, when I was a hospice chaplain, I would sometimes work with people with AIDS. And I had this one patient—his partner called me in to talk to him—who was having terrible nightmares about going to hell after he died. He had been raised in North Carolina, in a very fear-based, judgment-based church; and as soon as he realized he was gay, and was old enough to leave home, he did. And he never looked back.

And now he was in his fifties—and my part was to represent the faith community to him, and to speak the word of God's love to him, and to let myself be the vessel of that news rather than trying to step into God's place. I think the sinfulness comes in when we just want to be God, when we want to silence God. And there's plenty of scriptural basis for that definition of sin.

The passage that he loved was from Romans 8 where *nothing:*

> . . . neither death, nor life, nor angels
> . . . nor height, nor depth, nor any other

creature, shall be able to separate
us from the love of God . . .
                    —Romans 8:38-39

He had me read that to him constantly. He'd sleep
then wake up, and then read that again. He had asked
me, "Am I a sinner—because of this—just because of
who I am?" And I could say, "No," and assure him of
that. And it was because of those people in that chat
room.

Homosexuality, I don't think it is God's intent. But there are many, many things that are not God's intent that we are still doing.

Interesting. I've never associated "Love the sinner; hate the sin" with gay people. The first time I read this phrase, I was pretty young. But it refers to Christians. Christian sinners. Within the Church circle. You have to love your brothers and sisters even though they make mistakes, and continue to lead sinful lives.

I think the main passage for me is the Romans verse, chapter 1,[25] including those things that are not favorable to God. Up to now, I confirm that passage; I mean, my interpretation of it. But I'm open to correct myself.

I'm still open to the fact that some people are born homosexual. I think that's another issue. But if it is acquired, if it is a learned behavior—but some people, they don't have a choice.

I don't think I'm in a position—I dare not point my finger at one person and say, "You are a sinner." I don't do that, because I understand myself as a sinner. I am responsible for my own life. But also, I have the responsibility to help my fellow Christians live out their faith. But even though they may not do what I think is right, the bottom line is I have to respect people as they are.

And homosexuality, I don't think it is God's intent. But there are many, many things that are not God's intent that we are still doing. We lie to ourselves; we lie to other people, all the time. So we have to love the sinner if we are going to love ourselves. Because I'm a sinner.

To me, the most important thing is that the Gospel, the Good News, is talking about the redemptive love of God.

If you felt like expressing disapproval about homosexuality, you had to do it in an intimate, face-to-face way, in a relationship with somebody you cared about.

Back in 1994, I was attending a gathering of the evangelical branch of my denomination. I was one of the representatives from my church. And they were considering the approval of a statement renouncing same-sex marriage.

And our church had had a discussion about it, and there was a diversity of feelings about it, but unity on the idea that "renunciation," being so negative, was really an inappropriate way to take a public stand on the issue. So as the representative, I was freed by my church to express that, if I felt led. So I stood up.

I told them you should first go and talk to the people you disagree with, and get to know them, make friends with them if possible. And then, if you felt disapproval about homosexuality, and felt led to express that, you had to do it in an intimate, face-to-face way, in a relationship with somebody that you cared about. And their Statement of Renunciation was the opposite of that. But the discussion was like, "Oh, we totally agree with you, Beth. But 'Love the sinner; hate the sin.'"

And so when I get the call from Peggy saying there's this dialogue, it was like God tapping me on the back.

LISA

There is inclusion, there is love, there is welcoming, and then, all of a sudden: WHAM!

Once a year, Bobby, the minister who ran the boat shop, had this sermon that he read. It was by William Sloane Coffin[26] who, in regards to gay stuff, differentiates between several groups of Christians, some who say, "Absolutely! No problem!" and some who say, "Absolutely not! No acceptance, no anything!" And then, there's the middle group who says, "Okay, we understand that they're here and everything, but we don't want to talk about it."

And my response was to get really pissed off about that middle group. I'm sick and tired of wondering where people's boundaries are going to be.

My experience of that feels like being blindsided. Like there is inclusion, there is love, there is welcoming, and then, all of a sudden, WHAM: "That sticker is embarrassing" or "That t-shirt is inappropriate" or "These books, I don't want my kids reading these books." That, to me, is one of the least trustful positions to come up against.

When it comes down to it, it's just not a sin for me. And there's just no compromise there. There's no fuzziness.

And when opposition is readily apparent, I know what to do with it. But when it shows up in this "middle group," it's more disappointing to me.

MARGARET

I think both these sayings are bunk. They give people permission to be mean.

It seems to me, that what we have in Jesus—the easiest metaphor being his table fellowship—is a call to love. Which is enormously hard.

I find that it's really difficult to pray for people I disagree with. Last night, we prayed for George Bush, Dick Cheney, and John Ashcroft.[27] I don't think I have the courage to pray for those three by myself. It was good to be in a group because there is a call to care for your enemies.

It is a hugely hard thing to be open, to be in respectful dialogue with people, to learn who they are. And my job is to learn how to be loving. That seems like enough to do.

This "hate the sin" makes no sense. Because as soon as you hate the sin, you take on judgment which is God's job. So immediately you become blind. And I think both these sayings: "Love the sinner; hate the sin" and "Tell the truth in love" are bunk. They give people permission to be mean.

*Where are the avenues of love if we are always putting
people in boxes?*

I would like to talk about conscience. And the formation of conscience. For me, conscience is a process of prayer, of meaning, of listening. It's not just something that I've been taught, my conscience; it's something that I have to live with, that I have to live *by*. It's about how I want to be treated by others and how I will treat others.

So when I hear things like "Love the sinner; hate the sin," I feel like dialogue is very short-lived. Where are the avenues of love if we are always putting people in boxes?

One thing I know about God is that God's box is bigger. As soon as we put God into a box, we have limited that God-experience. And so, for me, I hear "Love the sinner; hate the sin" and I say that they are not seeing God opening. He is opening himself up to all of us.

PEGGY

I'm just waiting for the first gay person to say that she felt loved by a Christian wielding that language.

Love the sinner; hate the sin. Where do I start with this? I have never felt loved by anybody using this line. And the same thing comes to mind with the line, "Speak the truth in love." I am just waiting for the first gay person to say that she felt loved by a Christian wielding that language.

I did have a few years of going, *Oh yeah? Watch this!* then grabbing the Bible by the barrel and cocking it. But in recent years, I have to say that my conscience has led me to try and understand the other perspective. In such a way that I might be able to *find* the love.

I think that people who use the Bible in this way, use the Bible in this way categorically and not just to me. I've tried to understand that. Because if I focus on understanding, rather than the fact that they appear to be hating me, I can stay out of anger and hate, as well as the desire to return it. And that helps *me.*

STEVE

He never came back to church after that. For the rest of his life.

I was just remembering a friend of mine in the teen group. He went to my high school. His name was Jerry. The pastor's wife caught him smoking outside the church one day. She read him the riot act. I couldn't say very much because I was a teenager and she was the pastor's wife and she knew everything.

So I just said, "I didn't really feel like you handled that very well. Because now he's gone. He's not coming to church." And I don't remember if she actually said, "Love the sinner; hate the sin" but it was something to do with love. And he never came back to church after that. For the rest of his life.

And when I hear that phrase now, it doesn't seem to be happening in relationship. It's someone coming in on a website and saying *I know the answers*. They feel like they have the responsibility to point out sin. But they don't seem to feel the responsibility to love. That part of the phrase doesn't seem to click.

It's almost like the phrase comes right out of Scripture; but there is nothing in Scripture that says this, no Bible verse that says this.

Anyway, after I went my way and Jerry went his way, it was only after he was dying of AIDS, that his mother, who was still part of that church, wanted a minister to come to the house and pray for her son. And because the current minister at my home church wouldn't go, I was called in—and I met my old friend.

KAREN

We reject God when we put ourselves in God's place.

My understanding of what sin is, biblically, is our tendency to put ourselves in God's place, to try to be God instead of letting God be God. So it's when we get judgmental or when we think that we have the power of life and death over other people, when we get to decide who's righteous and who's not. I feel all these things fall into God's purview rather than ours. And so we reject God when we put ourselves in God's place.

BETH

Somebody put this little card on my windshield that said, "You whore."

When I was in law school, I used to commute with a group of three other women. I drove this beat-up old 1965 Volkswagen with a pro-choice bumper sticker on it. And one day, I went into the parking lot, and somebody had put this little card on my windshield that said, "You whore."

And I had settled down by then. I mean, there were other times in my life when I could have gone, *Well, yeah,* but at that time, there was no reason that I was aware of, except the bumper sticker.

And so it was this feeling of being attacked, misunderstood. And that's what this slogan reminds me of. Because "Love the sinner; hate the sin" can be experienced by others the way that I experienced that note.

Take 'the log' out of your own eye . . .

You know, when Jesus was on the cross, he didn't hate. Deal with your own sin first. That's the teaching of Jesus Christ. Take 'the log' out of your own eye so you can see clearly.[28]

BETH

It's the most frustrating thing if you are an evangelical. You can watch the whole thing devolve in front of your very eyes.

I think I truly believe the Scriptures. The Bible says we're all sinners. And I get really upset when people try to rank sins. Because if homosexuality is a sin, it's certainly no more sinful than anything that I am doing (the materialism). And to a great extent, I think that the revelation of sin has to be between you and God.

I wasn't raised evangelical. But I have spoken to evangelicals who, as youths, had it impressed upon them that, if they didn't save you and you went to hell, it was their fault. And they only had a little bit of time. And so there is this burden, this counterproductive burden that evangelicals are saddled with, that means it's their responsibility to save you—right now.

And they are trained to believe that, somehow, because of the power inherent in certain phrases, you'll get it! Which of course is simply not the case! Where there is no previous relationship and no actual love going on, it's the most frustrating thing if you are an evangelical. You can watch the whole thing devolve in front of your very eyes.

KAREN

If a relationship is just and loving then it is biblical.

A couple of years ago, my denomination did a big study on human sexuality in general. In our effort to try to find some sort of biblical ethic around sexuality—which many of us thought was fairly impossible due to some of the stories that are in there—the conclusion we came to was: if a relationship is just and loving then it is biblical. It fits into the biblical ethos.

We didn't say anything about whether the relationship was within marriage or outside of marriage, whether it was gay or straight.

Is the relationship just? Is the relationship loving?

It was soundly rejected by the national church. It was like, "No, no, no, no, no!" It was "way too fuzzy." And it didn't hold people to what they thought was a biblical standard.

I think "justice and love" is a very high biblical standard.

I don't expect things to happen overnight. It didn't happen to me overnight.

I am thinking about an academic paper written by a well-respected evangelical scholar, a gay-friendly paper that I forwarded to my sister. My sister asked her pastor whether or not it would be all right for her to read this paper. After the conversation, she decided against it.

I have a degree in physics and math and I want to hear all sides of an issue. You try this but you allow other possibilities, other hypotheses. But it happened over decades. This didn't happen coming right out of the teen group.

And even though I look at a lot of things that people in my denomination aren't willing to look at, these are the people I grew up with. I just know that they love God. So I have a great love for my church. It's frustrating at times, but there's a real sincerity in the midst of all that, a sincerity of faith.

The joy is to invite people to think about things a little differently. I teach ethics classes and allow the other point of view to be heard. But I don't expect things to happen overnight. It didn't happen to me overnight.

The Prodigal Daughter's Son

At any minute, it would all come screeching to a great-big, steel-sparking halt. Butter Cream cakes off of triple-parked vans; Sweet-on-You roses from Canadians; bubbling-at-the-mouth champagne from Parisians; heart-shaped chocolates on silver trays by singing waiters; gay people wearing everything from long white veils to mud-caked boots. Conservative Christian groups, arguing that a gay couple's wedding vows were a blow to their own connubial holiness, headed straight for the courts. Until then, it was a week of Valentine's Days at San Francisco City Hall—where I had raised my right hand, where I had just been sworn in, where I was about to speak the forbidden words.

Fearing ballot box repercussions, Mayor Newsom was pressured, begged not to do it—not now. But who could have predicted, in his gift to the gay community of San Francisco, the response by gay couples from Bangkok to Santiago?

They came with what they had on. They brought no witnesses; they brought no ministers; they brought no translators. They got off the airplanes and they all made a beeline for the party that wound like Christmas lights all the way around the block.

I hadn't seen a dry eye in two days—and never wept so much as I did when I said the words, "I now pronounce you spouses for life."

And I wept every time I heard them repeated: by those two women from Salt Lake City, who had raised two sons and been together twenty years before they said, "I give you this ring in token and pledge;" by the big wet eyes on that great big man as he promised his partner "constant faith and abiding love;" and by those two young women from Thailand—until something, mid-ceremony, told me to stop.

I turned to their bilingual witness. It was he to whom I read the vows, and he who repeated them, in his native tongue, to the two Thai women. Facing each other, it was they who said, "With this ring, I thee wed" in the language they'd shared all of their lives.

• • •

When my mother reported, the next day, that my nephew was on the interstate, and that we were all taking him to lunch, I wasn't ready, as he slip-knotted his spaghetti, to hear him describe the woman with whom I had just gotten off the phone. Here was Zachary braiding his noodles—he appeared to know Nora— but until my hamburger did a backflip off my lower lip, I didn't know that a burning interest had led him straight to the Pentecostal I'd asked to help me plot a course for the maiden voyage of First Be Reconciled.

Suffice it to say that my nephew had found a friend in Nora Nash. Suffice it to say, when Zachary told her he was gay, that he was speaking to a woman who— before FBR—believed gay Christians "needed to be converted."

Unlike the tired decree about "homosexuals" who "hate the Lord," or the declaration of my sister's friend that "Satan dances in their filth," Nora Nash gently christened and fully honored Zachary's love for God. "If I ever helped him," she would later tell me, "it was by believing in him, by counting him as a brother." First Be Reconciled had come full circle.

But that's not where it started for my nephew.

His scholarly venture into the works of Chaucer had failed to produce the fruits for which he had reached. But it had produced a messenger in the form of a roommate named Rick with whom Zachary had one life-changing conversation. Like Siddhartha stepping free of his royal stirrups and princely robes, it was the conversation through which my sister's son entered a world that had been denied.

"Those nine verses in the Bible?" Rick began. "Like the one in which the rape of two women—by a band of 'homosexual' men—precedes the godly wrath in which infants and old people are burned alive?" Home-schooled and house-churched, the Zachary I knew had never heard such talk.

"The god who is said to cast the blame," Rick went on, "not on the father who offers his daughters to a gang of rapists—but on a bunch of gay men?" With a flick of his wrist, Rick, future Presbyterian minister, tossed one view of Scripture over his shoulder. And with it, chapter and verse, went the anti-gay passages that Zachary wore like a hair shirt.

By the time Zach sat across the table from me and my hamburger, eight more Reconcilers had wrapped up twelve months of dialogue. By the time eleven states had lined up to restrict marriage vows to hetero-sexuals, Zachary had left the university for a seminary. By the time the wedding bell glee at San Francisco City Hall had given way to the ballot box victory of George Bush and Karl Rove, Zachary had become a gay evangelical seeking to remain true to the only god he knew.

But first he would post that Craigslist notice for a fourth Christian roommate. And first—as the pilot group of Reconcilers assembled for the first time—Nora Nash would ask her fellow peacemakers, "What does love look like?"

Six days later, a 747 sliced into a tall building. On the morning before the second session of FBR, a plane full of passengers, like a freight train on a high wire, etched the silhouettes of unnamed people, reaching for hands and leaping through flames, onto the Manhattan skyline.

Before the week was out, after taxiing half the Reconcilers over a bridge described as "a prime terrorist target," Nora would say the words I had never imagined I needed to hear. Not the words that I would have used to bless the journey of a friend, "Peggy," she said, "I see that you love God."

Before the year was out, Zachary would be raiding his refrigerator with a future Presbyterian minister. Reaching for the mayonnaise, his new roommate, Rick, the day he waved an exegetic wand over nine passages in Scripture, grabbed the mustard first. Arms full of condiments, he wrote off a handful of Bible quotes to "mere homophobia."

And after a lifetime of beaming like a lamp behind a bushel, that was it. That was all it took.

Like the heart that burst in his faithful horse when

Siddhartha set forth alone on foot; like the disgrace dreaded by the king when the prince returned with his begging bowl, one thing was clear: biblical sticks and scriptural stones would surely greet the coming out of this first born son. Yet, inside my nephew, a door opened through which morning entered. Like a cat stretches into the ray of light that warms a streak of winter floor, he fell asleep in a lick of sun and woke to find that he had let it in.

Notes

1. Guthrie, Woody. *This Land is Your Land*, 1944; publ. 1945 The Richmond Organization.

2. Philippians 4: 7

3. "Let anyone with ears to hear listen" Mark 4:9

4. Romans 1:26-27

5. Gender Inclusive Language balances male with female pronouns, or uses neutral pronouns, especially as they refer to the Divine.

6. Eddie "Gwen" Araujo, 1985–2002 was an American teenager who was murdered after it was discerned she was transgendered.

7. "God gave them up unto vile affections for even their women did change their natural use for that which is against nature."

8. Leviticus 20:13

9. *Welcome Back, Kotter*. ABC. September 1975. A situation comedy.

10. "Juan Luis Pedro Felipo de Huevos Epstein" played by actor Robert Hegyes. *Welcome Back, Kotter*. ABC. 1975

11. 1 Corinthians 14:33–35

12. 1 Timothy 2:12
13. Matthew 25:35–40
14. Dar Williams is an American singer-songwriter specializing in pop folk.
15. Williams, Dar. "When I Was a Boy." Lyrics. The Honesty Room. Razor and Tie. 1993
16. Genesis 16:13
17. Genesis 19:31–35
18. Judges 19:10–20:48
19. Luke 9:1–5
20. Mark 12:28-31
21. University of Chicago, 1980. Winner of the National Book Award and the Stonewall Book Award.
22. Boswell, John Eastburn, 1947–1994, a prominent Yale historian who focused on the relationship between religion and homosexuality.
23. Matthew 10:14
24. Hosea 1-14
25. Romans 1:26–32
26. An American clergyman and long-time peace activist until his death in 2006.
27. George Walker Bush, 43rd President of the United States (2001–2009); Richard Bruce Cheney, 46th Vice President (2001–2009); John David Ashcroft, United States Attorney General (2001–2005).
28. Matthew 7:3–5

Biblical References

Acknowledgments

I want to thank so many people for so many reasons. First, for their early and longstanding support of the project, "First Be Reconciled" (FBR), my deep gratitude goes to:

Rev. Ann B. Day of The E. Rhodes and Leona B. Carpenter Foundation, and to Rev. Dr. Riess Potterveld, President of the Graduate Theological Union, who was Vice President of Pacific School of Religion when FBR was learning to walk.

For their early, unflinching participation in the planning and co-facilitation of FBR, thanks and praise to my evangelical friends: Linda Bergquist, Steve Brown, Al Tizon, and my co-editor, Faith Jansen.

For his support and free advice, my thanks to Richard Smoley. For the fantastic cover design and typesetting, for his generosity and good humor, my gratitude to Drew Stevens. Deanna Horner, for the gracious, last-minute proofreading, thank you! Susan Hesse, for the expert eye since day one, bless you! Mimi Anzel, for ongoing feedback, Mirth on Earth!

For the support of students, staff and professors from the Graduate Theological Union, especially Bernard Schlager of Pacific School of Religion and the Center for Lesbian and Gay Studies, I wish to thank: John Davis, Nina Galvan, Speed Leas, Lizann Bassham, Jim Schaal, Mark Wilson, William O'Neill, Archie Smith, Timothy Tseng, Jerome Baggett, Steve Ellingson, Clare Fischer, Anita Cadonau-Huseby, Violeta de Rosas, Leah Sheppard, Gerald Brague and Jeramy Townsley.

For the support of the FBR Advisory Board members, not already mentioned above, I wish to thank: The Rt. Rev. William Swing, The Hon. Joanne O'Donnell, Fr. Gerald O'Rourke, Sister Ginny King, Dr. Frederic Luskin, Dr. Diana Whitney, Dr. Marjorie Schiller, and Prof. Cynthia Sampson.

For help above and beyond the call of duty, thank you, Brad Bunnin. For believing in the project and its mission, my thanks to Paul Chaffee. For Appreciative Inquiry, I am always grateful to David Cooperrider.

To all the people who participated in the dialogues, especially Margaret Alter, Steve Brown, Lisa Casey, Ed Mah, Edwin Mung, Beth Riley, and Karen Stokes, you guys are awesome! To all those I cannot name here because of our confidentiality agreement, you were fabulous. I love you all.

To those I have known since the Common Ground dialogues, like Kimberly Alvarenga, Amy Levine, and Shane Snowdon (who always appears when I need her) I'll never forget you. Thank you Joan Casamo and Linda Clarke, To Susan Levitz, to Stacey and Nathan, and to the women of the Susan B. Anthony Memorial Unrest Home for hosting my RV, my cat and me in your long shady driveways, thank you.

I'd like to thank my mom and dad for not laughing me off the edge of the earth for the two hundred years it took me to write this book. I want to thank my nephew for his tireless demonstration of good will. I am grateful to my two brothers for housing, diagnosing and repairing my RV, my cat and me while we hogged your long shady driveways. To my sister, for doing your best, thank you.

To my muse, Alix, who never left my side while I revised the first, second, third, fourth and fifth drafts, I miss you.

And finally, to my partner, Debi Mazor—who, in ten years, never once told me I should hurry up, finish up or give it up, but has, instead, put up with my moods, my sinuses, my memory lapses and humor lapses—thank you.

About the Author

PEGGY GREEN builds leadership teams across enemy lines. Contributing author of *Positive Approaches to Peacebuilding*, she has appeared on NPR, in newspapers coast to coast, and been recognized by Congress for Outstanding Community Service. She loves houseboats, hamburgers and bad cats. For engaging seminars and inspiring talks, visit PeggyGreen.net.